Baking Whoopies

The Seasonal Guide to Whoopie Pies

Polly Pomfrey

First published in Great Britain by Indepenpress

All paper used in the printing of this book has been made from wood grown in managed, sustainable forests.

ISBN13: 978-1-78003-015-9

Printed and bound in the UK
Indepenpress Publishing Limited
25 Eastern Place
Brighton
BN2 1GJ

A catalogue record of this book is available from the British Library

Design - Nicole Greatrex
Art director - Claire Spinks
Photographs - Richard Gailey
Marmite® is a trade mark of Unilever. Image (p.16) used by kind permission.

Contents

Foreword

The Power of the Whoopie Pie

When Polly first approached me about her ideas for a whoopie pie cookery book, I was taken aback - not only by her creative recipes and industrious drive to compile them into a volume, but also by her country of origin, the United Kingdom.

Having studied at the University of St Andrews for four years, Scotland and the UK remain dear to my heart. As a native New Englander and baker by profession, whoopie pies are perhaps even dearer. It made me smile that my favorite American treat has finally made its way to my second home. The fact that Polly is at the forefront of championing their introduction to the UK - perfecting flavors such as raspberry and cream, and mocha - was frosting on the pie, so to speak!

Just as Polly and Polly's Patisserie work as diplomats for all things whoopie pie in the UK, I've also been working to establish a bakery devoted to whoopie pies in my nation's capital, Washington DC.

Even in their home country, more often than not my customers approach my treats with some initial confusion, and many questions. "What's a whoopie pie? Is it a sandwich? Is it a cake? A cookie?" After listening to their queries over many months, I finally found my answer: A whoopie pie is anything you want it to be.

Whoopie pies have the shape of a cookie, the feel of a pie, and the flavors of a cake; all rolled up in one little sandwich of delight. While some of my customers are already familiar with whoopies, having grown up with them in New England, I find more often that those who have never before seen the baked goods are the people most delighted by their endearing qualities. Many fall instantly in love with them.

Given my own experience heralding the power of the whoopie pie to Washington DC, I guess I can't be that surprised by their popularity abroad. Cake, cookie, sandwich, pie - a delicacy by any other name would taste as sweet.

I wish Polly the best of luck in her quest to spread the whoopie word across two continents. Armed with her lovingly made pies, I can think of no more formidable ambassador.

McKee Floyd

Owner of Whoops!
Washington DC
www.whoopsbakeshop.com

Acknowledgements

A massive thank you to everyone who has helped me on my whoopie adventure!

There isn't room to name all of you, but in particular:

Matt - lots of love and support, and help in the kitchen when it all went a little nuts; Nancy, my expert kidnapper and whoopie spotter - and naughty little sister; my Chief Tasters - you know who you are; Richard Gailey, for taking amazing photos and having a Harry Potter window; Kate at Steamer Trading (Lewes), for lending beautiful equipment to use as props; Claire Wilson at Riverside Flowers (Lewes), for lending us lovely flowers and props; McKee Floyd of Whoops! Bakeshop: my whoopie sister, all the best with your whoopie adventuring; Nicole Greatrex, for her wonderful page design; and everyone at Indepenpress for being as enthusiastic as me, especially Claire Spinks for being discerning in all the right ways!

Introduction

Polly Pomfrey

Whoopie pies - also known as moon pies, gobs or BFOs (big fat Oreos) - are, like many things in the UK, an American import. For me, the enigma surrounding their origin is what first caused them to stand out from the crowd.

Their sandwich concept is familiar in established treats such as Viennese whirls, macarons and even the humble custard cream. However, the taste and texture of whoopies totally set them apart; not quite spongey but not quite biscuity, and loaded with plenty of moist filling. Get the flavour combination right and they taste like little drops of heaven.

Since their rapid rise in popularity in the UK, many supermarkets have begun selling them. Here, however, I would exercise a word of caution for whoopie lovers; although they look like the real thing and some taste almost like the real thing, a lot of them don't. At *all*. Artificial colours, glutinous textures and sickly sweet flavours combine to make it a less than satisfying and sadly underwhelming experience. Your best bet is to bake them yourself, or find a bakery that makes them fresh. The difference is amazing, and more than worth the extra effort or cost.

I'm assuming, since you are reading this book, that you are in the first camp and keen to get baking! You can, of course, skip straight to the recipes. If, like me, however, you are curious to know more about these delicious little treats, then read on...

The Origins of the Whoopie

By the time I had baked my own first batch of whoopies, I was curious to know more about their story - where on Earth had they sprung from? I first read about them in a magazine article, after which it seemed they were suddenly everywhere - on the television and radio, and in newspapers. Everyone was talking about them - an invasion had begun! But a little research uncovered only further questions. I discovered that as with all good traditions there was no single, infallible truth about their origin, except that they almost certainly came from North America, and that they probably emerged in the very early 20th century.

4

The widely held opinion is that whoopie pies originated in the Amish communities of America, specifically Pennsylvania. Made from leftover batter, it was said that when husbands and children found these treats in their lunchboxes they would shout "whoopie!" - hence the name. Migrating Amish, travelling to settlements across New England, naturally took the whoopie with them and so their reach and popularity quickly spread.

Another theory is that they originated in Boston, Massachusetts, via the company Durkee-Mower Inc. It's said the firm developed and included the whoopie pie in a collection of recipes entitled the *Yummy Book* to increase sales of its product, Marshmallow Fluff. But this rumour has since been discredited by employees of the company; according to them, although the *Yummy Book* of the 1970s did include a recipe for whoopie pies, the original 1930s edition did not.

There is an abundance of legends throughout Maine and Massachusetts about the birth of whoopies, with residents from both states proudly insisting their local bakery was responsible for the invention. Unfortunately, these claims result in more mystery and cannot be verified because the bakeries concerned have long since gone out of business or the company records have been destroyed.

Personally, I prefer the Amish story. The idea of Amish people spreading their simple cakes throughout New England, and from there the world, appeals greatly. Admittedly, though, this does appear at odds with the Amish ethos, so perhaps it's the romantic in me that favours this version of events. Wherever they came from, whoopie pies have well and truly arrived on our shores. Whether you enjoy them as tradition demands - simple, bare-naked whoopies - or whether you prefer a more modern, experimental approach, I feel certain that, once tried, you'll be completely hooked.

Whoopie Pie Flavours

Traditionally, whoopie pies were flavoured with cocoa and filled with marshmallow fluff. Nowadays, however, all sorts of whoopie concoctions are springing up. After focusing on the creation of new, sweet whoopie recipes, I began to wonder about other possibilities for the moreish little invaders. And since I've always leaned more towards the savoury, I sent my creative thoughts in that direction.

The first savoury whoopie I created was spinach and olive (page 24). My crop of spinach had matured, and I had a wealth of olives left over in the fridge. They were delicious! Savoury whoopies are very versatile and can be used as hors d'œuvres or appetisers at dinner parties or corporate functions. Or why not pack them in the hamper for a tasty picnic alternative? Or maybe include them as part of an ultra-modern wedding buffet? A far more inventive and original option to the retro vol-au-vent; they'll certainly pique the guests' curiosity!

Another fantastic way to use savoury whoopie pies is in children's lunchboxes. With no sugar and very little fat they can make a nutritious and appealing lunchtime snack for kids. To save time, you can bake a couple of giant, savoury whoopies, slice into portions and pop in the freezer until needed.

The recipes included in this book - with the exception of the original whoopie recipe - are the results of countless hours experimenting in my own kitchen with an assortment of ingredients, combinations and flavours. After vigorous testing on customers at my market stall as well as friends and members of my family, a few recipes didn't make it into this book. The ones that did received a unanimous thumbs-up from my volunteer tasters, and I hope you enjoy them as much as they did.

Whoopie Pie Sizes

Whoopie pies are usually 2-3" in diameter, and stuffed as thickly as possible with a filling. But don't let that stop you experimenting! You could create a giant whoopie birthday cake, or bite-sized whoopie treats. The table below shows the guidelines for baking different sizes:

Size of finished whoopie pie	Size to make batter	Yield from 1 standard batter mix	Baking time
Standard 2-3" (5-7cm)	2" rounds (5cm)	16-18 whoopies	10-12 mins
Giant 8" (20cm)	Two 6½-7" (16-18cm)	1 giant whoopie pie cake, plus a few spare standard	12-15 mins
Mini 1" (2.5cm)	¾" rounds (2cm)	35-40 whoopies	5-8 mins

Caring for Your Whoopie Pies

Unfilled, whoopies will keep in the fridge for about 4 days. Once they have been filled, however, it's best to eat them straight away, or within two days, depending on the filling. Use common sense to guide you; obviously, if you've used raw egg, for example, you won't be able to keep them for more than a day without risking serious food poisoning.

Storage

It's best to store whoopies in an airtight container. Be warned - if you are layering them on top of one another they will stick together. So it's a good idea to place a sheet of greaseproof or wax paper between the layers. They will probably still stick a little, but at least they won't be unsalvageable!

Freezing

Whoopie pies can be frozen - yippee! They will keep unfilled for up to a month in the freezer, in an airtight, freezer-proof container. Again, due to their sticky nature it's best to layer them with greaseproof or wax paper. They may freeze filled too, depending on the filling.

Fillings

The fillings I've used for the whoopies in this book are suggestions based on my own, and my testers' personal taste. Don't be a slave to conformity; feel free to mix and match the ingredients, swap them around and even invent new whoopies. If you don't like a particular ingredient, for example, change it to one you do. The more you experiment, the more you'll come to know what works best for you. I've also included a section on extra fillings at the back to give you some ideas for creating your own recipes.

Whoopie Experiments

Do you prefer lemon and raspberry to lemon and strawberry (page 30) Then try it! Here are a few things I've discovered in the course of my exploration, which may also come in useful for your own:

•   Baking is like chemistry; it's all in the balance, and the actions and reactions of ingredients.

•   Try to keep a balanced ratio of wet and dry ingredients. For example, if you add melted chocolate, take away a comparable amount of buttermilk.

•   If you add acidic foods (fruit for example) to the whoopie pie mix, they will come out flatter. This is because the acid reacts with the raising agent (bicarbonate of soda), causing it to act too quickly, meaning the whoopies don't rise.

•   The colour of your batter doesn't necessarily reflect the colour of your finished whoopie. When I first mixed the raspberry and cream whoopie, the batter turned pink. Once baked, however, they had a decidedly bluish tinge. Not the most appetizing look!

•   If you decide to add food colouring to the batter to alter the colour of the whoopies, you will need to add quite a lot. But bear in mind that you need to keep the balance of wet and dry ingredients - so you may need to add slightly less buttermilk to keep the levels right.

Whoopie Pies for Vegans

Having worked in a vegetarian/vegan pub for many years - but being neither myself - I have a keen awareness of how to cater for veggies and vegans. I understand both how easy it is, and also how interesting and creative you can get with the ingredients. I kept this in mind for this book, including only a couple of recipes containing meat. Both can easily be made meat-free; veggie bacon bits can be substituted in the mushroom and bacon whoopie (page 44), and for the pea, ham and mint (page 32), simply leave out the ham.

To make whoopie pies vegan, simply replace the butter with soya margarine, and the buttermilk/cream with soya cream or other suitable vegan alternative. You can use egg replacement powder instead of eggs, or leave them out altogether. On one of the many late-night whoopie 'bakeathons' I conduct for my market stall, I accidentally baked a batch without eggs, and only realised my mistake when I moved on to bake the next batch and saw I still had a full box of eggs left on the side. The whoopies tasted - and behaved - absolutely fine. They still rose, and nothing was missing from the flavour. They were a touch less moist than my usual whoopies, but a good dollop of extra filling soon took care of that.

Most of the whoopie pie recipes in this book can be made vegan with very little effort, For example, substitute cheeses for vegan alternatives. In the case of the honey and lavender recipe (page 26), you could try making a syrup with a dark brown sugar like muscavado (simply boil equal amounts of water and sugar). It won't taste the same as honey, but it could provide an interesting alternative!

In the alternative fillings selection I've included notes to show which are either vegan already, or could be made vegan by using a substitute ingredient like vegan cream cheese, for example.

A Note on the Recipes, Measurements and Temperatures

The whoopie pie recipes are arranged in a seasonal, month-by-month order. I've always preferred to cook in step with the seasons; the food has more flavour and is often more abundant and therefore cheaper. In this age of greater environmental consciousness and awareness of the carbon footprint created by flying out-of-season fruits and vegetables across the globe, seasonal cooking makes sense.

However, there is a little poetic licence here and there, which I hope will be forgiven. I've included strawberries in February's recipe, since it was created as a St Valentine celebration, and strawberries are associated with love. Not an issue for those of you with green-houses and green fingers, who can simply grow your own! As mentioned previously, one of the aims of this book is to encourage creative experimentation in whoopie pie baking. Therefore, the choice of which ingredients to include or omit will ultimately be down to your own taste as well as conscience.

The order of the recipes in this book is based on UK seasons, so if you are baking in another time zone, or even another hemisphere, you will need to adjust this accordingly. For example, people in Australia may prefer refreshing lemon and strawberry (page 30) whoopies at Christmas, and warming rum and raisin (page 54) in June. It's up to you - the world's your whoopie!

Originally, the recipes were cooked according to the UK Imperial system (pounds and ounces), so follow this method to get the best results. I have also provided conversions to metric and the US cup system (thanks, Erin!). But it goes without saying that you must stick to one measuring system throughout each recipe. Mixing them up will create problems because they do not translate exactly.

The oven temperatures used in the recipes include almost all the possible permutations - standard electric (Fahrenheit and Centigrade), fan-assisted (Centigrade only) and gas. I have used the most standard conversion method for these temperatures. However, do check and follow the guidelines to your specific make of oven for certainty. Some fan-assisted oven manufacturers recommend reducing the temperature only slightly, by 10°C, to that of a standard electric oven, while others suggest a 20°C reduction. For Fahrenheit, this is different again.

To be on the safe side, consult the specific guidelines for your own make of oven, and always check the whoopie pies slightly earlier than the stated cooking time.

January

Original whoopie pie

Makes approximately 18
Preparation: 20 minutes
Cooking: 10 minutes
Total: 30 minutes

Ingredients

- 4.5oz/130g/½ cup (1 stick) butter
- 7oz/200g/1 cup castor sugar
- 1 medium egg, beaten
- 13oz/370g/3 cups plain flour
- 1oz/30g/2 tbsp cocoa powder
- 1¼ tsp bicarbonate of soda
- ½ tsp salt
- 9fl oz/270ml/1 cup buttermilk

For the filling

- 9oz/250g/5 cups (miniature) marshmallows
- 1 tbsp water

The original whoopie pies were lightly flavoured with cocoa and filled with marshmallow fluff.

Method

Preheat your oven to 170°c (160°c fan)/325°f/GM 3 and grease a large baking sheet. Cream together the butter and sugar then add the egg a bit at a time, stirring well to make a smooth, curdle-free mix.

Put the flour, cocoa, bicarbonate of soda and salt into a sieve, and have the buttermilk to hand. Sieve half the flour mixture into the butter mixture and fold in gently, then add half the buttermilk and mix well. Continue until all the flour and buttermilk is folded in and you have a smooth, thick batter.

Pipe (or dollop) the batter into 2" diameter rounds and smooth off with the back of a spoon. Bake in the oven for 10-12 minutes, until they spring back when lightly touched. When cooked, leave to cool in the tray for 5 minutes before transferring to a wire rack.

To make the marshmallow fluff filling...

You can buy ready-made marshmallow fluff from most shops in the US, some shops in the UK, and online. However, it is easy to make your own.

Place the marshmallows and water in a heatproof bowl and microwave gently to melt. Once melted, drain any excess water, then stir well and leave for 5 minutes until the marshmallow fluff begins to set.

Put two generous teaspoons of the fluff onto one whoopie and, if presentation is important, leave to set for 5 minutes so the marshmallow does not run. If not, press another whoopie on top immediately and sandwich together.

January

Cheesy leek whoopie pie

Makes approximately 16
Preparation: 10 minutes
Cooking: 10 minutes
Total: 20 minutes

Ingredients

- 7oz/200g/2¼ cups finely chopped leek
- 2oz/50g/½ cup grated cheddar cheese
- 8oz/225g/1¾ cups plain flour
- 1 tsp bicarbonate of soda
- 2.5oz/75g/¼ cup (½ stick) butter
- 7fl oz/200ml/¾ cup buttermilk
- 1 medium egg

For the filling

- Cheddar cheese, sliced

A delicious alternative to sandwiches, these savoury whoopies are perfect for any lunchtime occasion.

Method

Preheat your oven to 170°c (160°c fan)/325°f/GM 3 and grease a large baking sheet.

Finely chop the leek and place in a large mixing bowl, then grate the cheese on top.

Sift the flour and bicarbonate of soda into the bowl with the leek and cheese. Add all the other ingredients.

Mix well with an electric hand whisk or wooden spoon until you have a smooth, thick batter.

Pipe (or dollop) the whoopie pie batter into 2" diameter rounds then bake in the oven for 10-12 minutes, or until they spring back when lightly touched.

When cooked, take out of the oven and leave to cool in the tray for 5 minutes, before transferring to a wire rack.

For the filling...

Slice the cheese and sandwich between two whoopie halves.

Why not try...

Putting a slice of tomato in with the cheese?

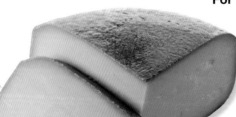

13

Double chocolate whoopie pie with strawberries and cream

Makes approximately 18
Preparation: 20 minutes
Cooking: 10 minutes
Total: 30 minutes

Ingredients

- 4.5oz/130g/½ cup (1 stick) butter
- 7oz/200g/1 cup castor sugar
- 1 medium egg, beaten
- 11oz/310g/2½ cups plain flour
- 3oz/85g/1 cup cocoa powder
- 1¼ tsp bicarbonate of soda
- ½ tsp salt
- 9fl oz/270ml/1 cup buttermilk
- 2oz/55g dark chocolate (70% cocoa if possible)

For the filling

- 4oz/115g/½ cup (1 stick) unsalted butter
- 8oz/225g/2 cups (unsifted) icing sugar
- 1 tbsp milk
- ½ tsp vanilla essence

For the topping

- 5fl oz/150ml/½ cup double or whipping cream
- 14oz/400g/2½ cups whole strawberries

A decadent, delicious St Valentine's dream... swoon!

Method

Preheat your oven to 170°c (160°c fan)/325°f/GM 3 and grease a large baking sheet. Break the chocolate into small pieces and gently melt in a microwave or a heatproof bowl on top of a saucepan of simmering water (do not allow the water to come into contact with the chocolate). Once melted, set to one side to cool slightly.

Cream together the butter and sugar, then add the egg, a bit at a time, stirring well to make a smooth, curdle-free mix. Put the flour, cocoa, bicarbonate of soda and salt into a sieve, and have the buttermilk and melted chocolate to hand. Sieve half the flour mixture into the butter mixture. Fold in gently, add half the melted chocolate and mix well, then add half the buttermilk. Continue until all the flour, chocolate and buttermilk is folded in and you have a smooth, thick batter.

Pipe (or dollop) the whoopie pie batter into 2" diameter rounds. Smooth off with the back of a spoon and bake in the oven for 10-12 minutes, or until they spring back when lightly touched, then leave to cool in the tray for 5 minutes before transferring to a wire rack.

To make the vanilla buttercream filling...

Beat the butter with a wooden spoon or electric whisk until light and creamy. Add half the icing sugar and mix well. Tip the remaining icing sugar into the bowl and beat until the buttercream is creamy. Add the milk and vanilla and mix well.

Bringing it all together...

Whip the cream with an electric whisk until it forms stiff peaks, and slice the strawberries. Spoon a dollop of cream onto each whoopie, and place a strawberry slice on top.

15

February

Cheddar and Marmite® whoopie pie

Makes approximately 18-20
Preparation: 10 minutes
Cooking: 10 minutes
Total: 20 minutes

Ingredients

- 7oz/200g/1¾ cups grated cheddar cheese
- 8oz/225g/1¾ cups plain flour
- 1 tsp bicarbonate of soda
- 2.5oz/75g/¼ cup (½ stick) butter
- 7fl oz/200ml/¾ cup buttermilk
- 1 medium egg

For the filling

- 7oz/200g/¾ cup cream cheese
- 3-4 tsp Marmite®

Serve these easy-to-make whoopie pies for the perfect British snack.

Method

Preheat your oven to 170°c (160°c fan)/325°f/GM 3 and grease a large baking sheet.

Finely grate the cheese into a large mixing bowl, then sift the flour and bicarbonate of soda on top of the cheese.

Add all the other ingredients and mix well with an electric hand whisk or wooden spoon until you have a smooth, thick batter.

Pipe (or dollop) the whoopie pie batter into 2" diameter rounds and smooth off with a spoon.

Bake in the oven for 10-12 minutes, or until they spring back when lightly touched.

When cooked, take out of the oven and leave to cool in the tray for 5 minutes, before transferring to a wire rack.

To make the filling...

Mix the Marmite® in with the cream cheese. Spread the mixture thickly on one whoopie half then place the other on top.

Why not try...

Adding some finely chopped celery or spring onion to the cream cheese and Marmite® filling?

Mocha whoopie pie with mascarpone

Makes approximately 18
Preparation: 20 minutes
Cooking: 10 minutes
Total: 30 minutes

Ingredients

- 4.5oz/130g/½ cup (1 stick) butter
- 7oz/200g/1 cup castor sugar
- 1 medium egg, beaten
- 12oz/340g/2½ cups plain flour
- 2oz/55g/½ cup cocoa powder
- 1¼ tsp bicarbonate of soda
- ½ tsp salt
- 7fl oz/200ml/¾ cup buttermilk
- 3 tbsp water mixed with 3 tbsp instant coffee

For the filling

- 7oz/200g/¾ cup mascarpone cheese
- 1 tsp cocoa
- 1 tsp instant coffee mixed with 1 tsp water

These richly flavoured coffee hits work well as mini after-dinner whoopies – perfect with a glass of red wine.

Method

Preheat your oven to 170°c (160°c fan)/325°f/GM 3 and grease a large baking sheet. Cream together the butter and sugar then add the egg a bit at a time, stirring well to make a smooth, curdle-free mixture.

Put the flour, bicarbonate of soda and salt into a sieve, and have the buttermilk and coffee mixture to hand.

Sieve half the flour mixture into the butter mixture and fold in gently, then add half the buttermilk and half the coffee mixture and stir well.

Continue to stir until all the flour, buttermilk and coffee is folded in, and you have a smooth, thick batter.

Pipe (or dollop) the whoopie pie batter into 2" diameter rounds and smooth off with the back of a spoon.

Bake in the oven for 10-12 minutes, or until they spring back when lightly touched.

When cooked, take the whoopies out of the oven and leave to cool in the tray for 5 minutes, before transferring to a wire rack.

To make the mascarpone filling...

Place the mascarpone in a bowl then add the coffee and chocolate and mix well.

19

march

Pesto and cream cheese whoopie pie

Makes approximately 16
Preparation: 10 minutes
Cooking: 10 minutes
Total: 20 minutes

Ingredients

- 8oz/225g/1¾ cups plain flour
- 1 tsp bicarbonate of soda
- 2.5oz/75g/¼ cup (½ stick) butter
- 7fl oz/200ml/¾ cup buttermilk
- 1 medium egg
- 5 heaped teaspoons of either green or red pesto

For the filling

- 7oz/200g/¾ cup cream cheese
- 2-3 tsp green or red pesto

Add a dash of Italian flavour to your day with these tasty pesto treats.

Method

Preheat your oven to 170°c (160°c fan)/325°f/GM 3 and grease a large baking sheet.

Sift the flour and bicarbonate of soda into a large mixing bowl, then add all the other ingredients.

Mix well with an electric hand whisk or wooden spoon until you have a smooth, thick batter.

Pipe (or dollop) the whoopie pie batter into 2" diameter rounds and smooth off with a spoon.

Bake in the oven for 10-12 minutes, or until they spring back when lightly touched.

When cooked, take out of the oven and leave to cool in the tray for 5 minutes, before transferring to a wire rack.

To make the filling...

Mix the cream cheese with the pesto. Spread the mixture thickly on one whoopie half, then place the other on top.

Why not try...

Adding crushed, toasted pine nuts to the cream cheese?

21

April

Hot cross whoopie pie

Makes approximately 18
Preparation: 20 minutes
Cooking: 10 minutes
Total: 30 minutes

Ingredients

- 4.5oz/130g/½ cup (1 stick) butter
- 7oz/200g/1 cup castor sugar
- 1 medium egg, beaten
- 14oz/395g/3 cups plain flour
- 7oz/200g/1½ cups (packed) raisins
- ½ tsp ground cinnamon
- ½ tsp ground ginger
- ½ tsp ground nutmeg
- 1¼ tsp bicarbonate of soda
- ½ tsp salt
- 9fl oz/270ml/1 cup buttermilk

For the crosses

- 3oz/85g/½ cup (¾ stick) butter
- 6oz/170g/1½ cups flour
- 1 tbsp water

For the filling

- Jam (whichever flavour you prefer)
- Butter

A twist on the traditional springtime favourite.

Method

Preheat your oven to 170°c (160°c fan)/325°f/GM 3 and grease a large baking sheet.

To make the crosses, rub the butter into the flour until it resembles fine breadcrumbs, then add the water and mix well to form a pastry dough. Roll out the dough to around 2mm thick and, using a knife, cut the pastry into thin strips about 5mm (¼ inch) thick. Put to one side.

Cream together the butter and sugar then add the egg a bit at a time, stirring well to make a smooth, curdle-free mixture. Put the flour, cinnamon, ginger, nutmeg, bicarbonate of soda and salt into a sieve, and have the buttermilk to hand. Sieve half the flour mixture into the butter mixture and fold in gently, then add half the buttermilk and mix well. Continue until all the flour and buttermilk is folded in, and you have a smooth, thick batter. Add the raisins and mix well.

Pipe (or dollop) the whoopie pie batter into 2" diameter rounds and smooth off with the back of a spoon. Take one strip of pastry, place horizontally across a whoopie and cut off any excess. Take another strip of pastry and place it vertically on the whoopie to form a cross. Again, cut off any excess.

Using a pastry brush, lightly brush the pastry crosses with milk. Repeat on all the whoopies then bake in the oven for 10-12 minutes, or until they spring back when lightly touched. When cooked, leave to cool in the tray for 5 minutes, before transferring to a wire rack.

Bringing it all together...

Spread butter and jam onto one whoopie half, then simply place the other whoopie half on top.

23

 April

Spinach and olive whoopie pie

Makes approximately 16
Preparation: 10 minutes
Cooking: 10 minutes
Total: 20 minutes

Ingredients

- 2oz/50g/1¾ cups fresh spinach
- 2oz/50g/20 individual pitted black olives
- 8oz/225g/1¾ cups plain flour
- 1 tsp bicarbonate of soda
- Small pinch of salt
- 2.5oz/75g/¼ cup (½ stick) butter
- 7fl oz/200ml/¾ cup buttermilk
- 1 medium egg

For the filling

- 7oz/200g/¾ cup cream cheese

Full of savoury flavour, these handy snack-sized treats are ideal for lunchboxes and hampers.

Method

Preheat your oven to 170°c (160°c fan)/325°f/GM 3 and grease a large baking sheet.

Finely chop the spinach and olives into a large, roomy mixing bowl, then sift the flour, bicarbonate of soda and salt on top.

Add all the other ingredients and mix well with an electric hand whisk or wooden spoon until you have a smooth, thick batter.

Pipe (or dollop) the whoopie pie batter into 2" diameter rounds and smooth off with a spoon.

Bake in the oven for 10-12 minutes, or until they spring back when lightly touched.

When cooked, take out of the oven and leave to cool in the tray for 5 minutes, before transferring to a wire rack.

For the filling...

Spread cream cheese generously on one whoopie half and sandwich together with the other.

Why not try...

Flavouring the cream cheese with fresh basil, or adding a little crumbled feta to the cream cheese?

 24

25

May Honey whoopie pie with lavender mascarpone filling

Makes approximately 18
Preparation: 20 minutes
Cooking: 10 minutes
Total: 30 minutes

Ingredients

- 4.5oz/130g/½ cup (1 stick) butter
- 8oz/226g/1 cups clear honey
- 1 beaten egg
- 14oz/395g/3 cups plain flour
- 1¼ tsp bicarbonate of soda
- ½ tsp salt
- 6fl oz/175ml/¾ cup buttermilk

For the filling

- 7oz/200g/1 cup mascarpone cheese
- 1oz/25g/½ cup mini honeycomb pieces
- 1 tsp fresh, finely chopped lavender

Delicate lavender notes hit the tongue first, followed by the smoothness of honey – sublime!

Method

Preheat your oven to 170°c (160°c fan)/325°f/GM 3 and grease a large baking sheet. Cream the butter until it is pale and fluffy, then pour the honey into the butter and beat well. Add the egg a bit at a time, stirring well to make a smooth, curdle-free mixture.

Put the flour, bicarbonate of soda and salt into a sieve. Sieve half the flour mixture into the butter mixture and fold in gently. Add half the buttermilk and mix well, continuing until all flour and buttermilk is folded in, and you have a smooth, thick batter.

Pipe (or dollop) the whoopie pie batter into 2" diameter rounds and smooth off with the back of a spoon. Bake in the oven for 10-12 minutes, or until they spring back when lightly touched. When cooked, take out of the oven and leave to cool in the tray for 5 minutes, before transferring to a wire rack.

To make the lavender mascarpone filling...

Take 1 freshly cut lavender head and chop finely. Add half the lavender and honeycomb pieces to the mascarpone and mix well, taste, then add more lavender as necessary. Too much too soon and it might taste like soap!

Notes on lavender...

- Make sure no pesticides, fungicides, fertilisers or other chemicals – anything that may be hazardous to health – have come into contact with the lavender bush. If in doubt, don't use it.
- Get permission from the person who owns the lavender bush before you pick any!

Sun-dried tomato and mozzarella whoopie pie

Makes approximately 16
Preparation: 10 minutes
Cooking: 10 minutes
Total: 20 minutes

Ingredients

- 8oz/225g/1¾ cups plain flour
- 1 tsp bicarbonate of soda
- 2.5oz/75g/¼ cup (½ stick) butter
- 7fl oz/200ml/¾ cup buttermilk
- 1 medium egg
- 3 pieces of sun-dried tomato (about 1oz/20g), finely diced
- 2 tsp tomato puree
- 1 tsp dried basil

For the filling

- 9oz/250g mozzarella, sliced (you may require a little more or less depending on thickness)

Celebrate the approaching summer with these delectable light bites.

Method

Preheat your oven to 170°c (160°c fan)/325°f/GM 3 and grease a large baking sheet.

Sift the flour and bicarbonate of soda into a large mixing bowl, then add all the other ingredients.

Mix well with an electric hand whisk or wooden spoon until you have a smooth, thick batter.

Pipe (or dollop) the whoopie pie batter into 2" diameter rounds and smooth off with a spoon.

Bake in the oven for 10-12 minutes, or until they spring back when lightly touched.

When cooked, take out of the oven and leave to cool in the tray for 5 minutes, before transferring to a wire rack.

For the filling...

Slice the mozzarella and sandwich between two whoopie halves.

Why not try...

Adding some fresh basil leaves to the whoopie sandwich?

28

June

Lemon whoopie pie with strawberry buttercream

Makes approximately 18
Preparation: 20 minutes
Cooking: 10 minutes
Total: 30 minutes

Ingredients

- 4.5oz/130g/½ cup (1 stick) butter
- 7oz/200g/1 cup castor sugar
- 1 medium egg, beaten
- 14oz/395g/3 cups plain flour
- 1¼ tsp bicarbonate of soda
- ½ tsp salt
- 8fl oz/230ml/1 cup buttermilk
- 2 tbsp lemon curd

For the filling

- 4oz/115g/½ cup (1 stick) unsalted butter
- 8oz/225g/2 cups (unsifted) icing sugar
- 2oz/55g/½ cup (whole) fresh strawberries, or 2-3 drops strawberry flavouring
- 1 tbsp milk (omit if using fresh strawberries)

Sweet strawberry buttercream perfectly complements the tart lemon whoopies.

Method

Preheat your oven to 170°c (160°c fan)/325°f/GM 3 and grease a large baking sheet. Cream together the butter and sugar, then add the egg a bit at a time, stirring well to make a smooth, curdle-free mixture.

Put the flour, bicarbonate of soda and salt into a sieve and have the buttermilk to hand. Gently heat the lemon curd in the microwave until slightly runny. This helps it to mix. Sieve half the flour mixture into the butter mix and fold in gently. Add half the buttermilk and half the lemon curd, and mix into a thick batter.

Pipe (or dollop) the batter into 2" diameter rounds and smooth off with the back of a spoon. Bake in the oven for 10-12 minutes, or until they spring back when lightly touched, then leave to cool for 5 minutes.

To make the strawberry buttercream filling...

Beat the butter with a wooden spoon or electric whisk until light and creamy. Add half the icing sugar and mix well. Tip the rest of the icing sugar into the bowl and beat until the buttercream is pale and creamy.

If you are using fresh strawberries...

Wash the strawberries and place in a jug or deep bowl. Using a hand blender, whizz to a puree then force through a sieve using a spoon. Add 1 tbsp of the puree to the buttercream and mix well.

If you are using strawberry flavouring...

Mix the milk and strawberry flavouring together. Add a drop of pink or red food colouring to turn the buttercream pink.

June

Pea, ham and mint whoopie pie

Makes approximately 16
Preparation: 10 minutes
Cooking: 10 minutes
Total: 20 minutes

Ingredients

- 3.5oz/100g/4 slices ham, diced
- 3.5oz/100g/¾ cup peas (fresh or frozen)
- 1 tbsp chopped fresh mint
- 8oz/225g/1¾ cups plain flour
- 1 tsp bicarbonate of soda
- 2.5oz/75g/¼ cup (½ stick) butter
- 7fl oz/200ml/¾ cup buttermilk
- 1 medium egg

For the filling

- 7oz/200g/¾ cup cream cheese
- 7oz/200g ham, roughly cut into pieces that will fit inside a whoopie pie

Perfect for picnics, these snack-sized whoopies provide a delicate taste of the best of British fare.

Method

Preheat your oven to 170°c (160°c fan)/325°f/GM 3 and grease a large baking sheet.

Dice the ham into smallish pieces and place in a large mixing bowl, along with the peas and chopped mint.

Sift the flour and bicarbonate of soda into the bowl with the peas, ham and mint, then add all the other ingredients.

Mix well with an electric hand whisk or wooden spoon until you have a smooth, thick batter.

Pipe (or dollop) the whoopie pie batter into 2" diameter rounds.

Bake in the oven for 10-12 minutes, or until they spring back when lightly touched.

When cooked, take out of the oven and leave to cool in the tray for 5 minutes, before transferring to a wire rack.

For the filling...

Spread the cream cheese on a whoopie half then place the ham and other whoopie half on top.

Why not try...

Chopping some fresh rocket and adding it to the cream cheese filling for a peppery zing?

32

Raspberry and cream whoopie pie

Makes approximately 18
Preparation: 20 minutes
Cooking: 10 minutes
Total: 30 minutes

Ingredients

- 4.5oz/130g/½ cup (1 stick) butter
- 7oz/200g/1 cup castor sugar
- 1 medium egg, beaten
- 14oz/395g/3 cups plain flour
- 1¼ tsp bicarbonate of soda
- ½ tsp salt
- 6fl oz/180ml/¾ cup single cream
- 5oz/150g/1½ cups fresh or frozen raspberries (to make raspberry puree for both whoopie batter and buttercream filling)

For the filling

- 4oz/115g/½ cup (1 stick) unsalted butter
- 8oz/225g/2 cups (unsifted) icing sugar
- 1 tbsp raspberry puree

Smooth and sophisticated, perfect with a glass of Pimm's for a classic English summer picnic.

Method

Preheat your oven to 170°c (160°c fan)/325°f/GM 3 and grease a large baking sheet.

To make the raspberry puree, place the raspberries in a sieve and, holding the sieve over a bowl, force the raspberries through using a spoon. Rinse the sieve straight away and put the bowl containing the raspberry puree to one side. You will use this to flavour both the whoopie batter and the buttercream.

Cream together the butter and sugar. Add the egg a bit at a time, stirring well to make a smooth, curdle-free mixture. Put the flour, bicarbonate of soda and salt into a sieve and mix 3 tbsp of raspberry puree into the buttermilk.

Sieve half the flour mixture into the butter mixture and fold in gently, then add half the buttermilk/raspberry mixture and stir well. Continue until you have a smooth, thick batter.

Pipe (or dollop) the whoopie pie batter into 2" diameter rounds and smooth off with the back of a spoon. Bake in the oven for 10-12 minutes, or until they spring back when lightly touched, then leave to cool in the tray for 5 minutes, before transferring to a wire rack.

To make the raspberry buttercream filling...

Beat the butter with a wooden spoon or electric whisk until light and creamy. Add about half the icing sugar, and mix well. Tip the remaining icing sugar into the bowl and continue to beat until the buttercream is pale and creamy. Add 1 tbsp of raspberry puree to the buttercream, and mix well.

Red pepper and goats' cheese whoopie pie

Makes approximately 16
Preparation: 10 minutes
Cooking: 10 minutes
Total: 20 minutes

Ingredients

- 2.5oz/75g/¼ cup (½ stick) butter
- 1 red pepper, chopped (about 7oz/200g/1½ cup)
- 1 generous tsp dried oregano
- 8oz/225g/1¾ cups plain flour
- 1 tsp bicarbonate of soda
- 7fl oz/200ml/¾ cup buttermilk
- 1 medium egg

For the filling

- 10oz/300g goats' cheese, sliced

Add some sunshine to your menu with these delicious summery treats.

Method

Preheat your oven to 170°c (160°c fan)/325°f/GM 3 and grease a large baking sheet.

Melt the butter and place in a large, roomy mixing bowl. Add the chopped pepper and oregano then whizz with a hand blender to make a rough puree.

Sift the flour and bicarbonate of soda on top of the puree, then add the egg and buttermilk. Mix well with an electric hand whisk or wooden spoon until you have a smooth, thick batter.

Pipe (or dollop) the whoopie pie batter into 2" diameter rounds.

Bake in the oven for 10-12 minutes, or until they spring back when lightly touched.

When cooked, take out of the oven and leave to cool in the tray for 5 minutes, before transferring to a wire rack.

For the filling...

Slice the goats' cheese and sandwich between two whoopie halves.

Why not try...

Adding some fresh thyme to the goats' cheese?

37

August

English rose whoopie pie

Makes approximately 18
Preparation: 20 minutes
Cooking: 10 minutes
Total: 30 minutes

Ingredients

- 4.5oz/130g/½ cup (1 stick) butter
- 7oz/200g/1 cup castor sugar
- 1 medium egg, beaten
- 14oz/395g/3 cups plain flour
- 1¼ tsp bicarbonate of soda
- ½ tsp salt
- 4fl oz/120ml/½ cup rosewater
- 5fl oz/150ml/1 cup buttermilk

For the filling

- 4oz/115g/½ cup (1 stick) unsalted butter
- 8oz/225g/2 cups (unsifted) icing sugar
- 1 tbsp rosewater

Delicately scented with roses, this whoopie pie is a wonderful addition to tea parties.

Method

Preheat your oven to 170°c (160°c fan)/325°f/GM 3 and grease a large baking sheet.

Cream together the butter and sugar, then add the egg a bit at a time, stirring well to make a smooth, curdle-free mixture. Put the flour, bicarbonate of soda and salt into a sieve, and have the buttermilk and rosewater to hand.

Sieve half the flour mixture into the butter mixture and fold in gently. Add half the buttermilk and half the rosewater, and mix well. Continue until all the flour, buttermilk and rosewater is folded in, and you have a smooth, thick batter.

Pipe (or dollop) the whoopie pie batter into 2" diameter rounds and smooth off with the back of a spoon.

Bake in the oven for 10-12 minutes, or until the whoopies spring back when lightly touched. When cooked, take out of the oven and leave to cool in the tray for 5 minutes, before transferring to a wire rack.

To make the rosewater buttercream filling...

Beat the butter with a wooden spoon or an electric whisk until light and creamy, then add about half the icing sugar and mix in well.

Tip the rest of the icing sugar into the bowl, mix and continue to beat until the buttercream is pale and creamy. Add the rosewater and mix well.

38

39

August

Feta and red onion whoopie pie

Makes approximately 16
Preparation: 10 minutes
Cooking: 10 minutes
Total: 20 minutes

Ingredients

- 8oz/225g/1¾ cups plain flour
- 1 tsp bicarbonate of soda
- 2.5oz/75g/¼ cup (½ stick) butter
- 7fl oz/200ml/¾ cup buttermilk
- 1 medium egg
- 2.5oz/75g/½ cup crumbled feta cheese
- 1 small red onion, finely chopped
- 1 tsp fresh thyme

For the filling

- 3.5oz/100g/½ cup cream cheese
- 3.5oz/100g/½ cup feta cheese

Make autumn's arrival more palatable with these deliciously strong flavoured whoopies.

Method

Preheat your oven to 170°c (160°c fan)/325°f/GM 3 and grease a large baking sheet.

Sift the flour and bicarbonate of soda into a large mixing bowl, then crumble the feta into the flour mix and add all the other ingredients.

Mix well with an electric hand whisk or wooden spoon until you have a smooth, thick batter.

Pipe (or dollop) the whoopie pie batter into 2" diameter rounds and bake in the oven for 10-12 minutes, or until they spring back when lightly touched.

When cooked, take out of the oven and leave to cool in the tray for 5 minutes, before transferring to a wire rack.

To make the filling...

Crumble the feta cheese into a mixing bowl, then add the cream cheese and stir well.

Why not try...

Adding a little lemon or lime zest to the cream cheese filling?

41

september

Carrot whoopie pie with orange cream cheese

Makes approximately 18
Preparation: 20 minutes
Cooking: 10 minutes
Total: 30 minutes

Ingredients

- 4.5oz/130g/½ cup (1 stick) butter
- 7oz/200g/1 cup castor sugar
- 1 medium egg, beaten
- 14oz/395g/3 cups plain flour
- 7oz/200g/1¾ cups grated carrot
- 1¼ tsp bicarbonate of soda
- ½ tsp salt
- ½ tsp ground cumin
- 9fl oz/270ml/1 cup buttermilk

For the filling

- 7oz/200g/1 cup cream cheese
- 1 orange

A novel adaptation of traditional carrot cake, these whoopies are a fun treat anytime.

Method

Preheat your oven to 170°c (160°c fan)/325°f/GM 3 and grease a large baking sheet.

Cream together the butter and sugar, then add the egg a bit at a time, stirring well to make a smooth, curdle-free mixture.

Put the flour, bicarbonate of soda, ground cumin and salt into a sieve, and have the buttermilk and carrot to hand.

Sieve half the flour mixture into the butter mixture and fold in gently. Add half the buttermilk, and mix well.

Continue until all flour and buttermilk is folded in, and you have a smooth, thick batter, then add the grated carrot, and mix well.

Pipe (or dollop) the whoopie pie batter into 2" diameter rounds and smooth off with the back of a spoon.

Bake in the oven for 10-12 minutes, until they spring back when lightly touched. When cooked, take out of the oven and leave to cool in the tray for 5 minutes, before transferring to a wire rack.

To make the orange cream cheese filling...

Put the cream cheese in a large bowl. Finely grate the orange rind, and add the zest to the cream cheese.

Beat well with an electric whisk.

42

september

Mushroom and bacon whoopie pie

Makes approximately 16
Preparation: 10 minutes
Cooking: 20 minutes
Total: 30 minutes

Ingredients

- 3.5oz/100g/1 cup (whole) mushrooms
- 8oz/225g/1¾ cups plain flour
- 1 tsp bicarbonate of soda
- 2.5oz/75g/¼ cup (½ stick) butter
- 7fl oz/200ml/¾ cup buttermilk
- 1 medium egg

For the filling

- 7oz/200g/¾ cup cream cheese
- 5-6 rashers of smoked, streaky bacon

A quick and easy alternative to your usual breakfast, brunch or mid-morning snack.

Method

Preheat your oven to 170°c (160°c fan)/325°f/GM 3 and grease a large baking sheet.

Put the mushrooms in a mixing bowl and whizz using a hand blender to create a mushroom puree.

Sift the flour and bicarbonate of soda on top of the mushroom puree, then add all the other ingredients. Mix well with an electric hand whisk or wooden spoon until you have a smooth, thick batter.

Pipe (or dollop) the whoopie pie batter into 2" diameter rounds and smooth off with the back of a spoon.

Bake in the oven for 10-12 minutes, or until they spring back when lightly touched.

When cooked, take out of the oven and leave to cool in the tray for 5 minutes, before transferring to a wire rack.

To make the filling...

Grill the bacon until it's nice and crispy all over. Leave to cool for a short while then crumble it into the cream cheese.

Why not try...

Adding a chopped spring onion to the bacon and cream cheese?

44

45

Pumpkin whoopie pie with homemade pecan ice cream

Makes approximately 18
Preparation: 20 minutes
Cooking: 10 minutes
Total: 30 minutes

Ingredients

- 4.5oz/130g/½ cup (1 stick) butter
- 7oz/200g/1 cup castor sugar
- 1 medium egg, beaten
- 14oz/395g/3 cups plain flour
- ½ tsp ground cinnamon
- ½ tsp ground nutmeg
- ½ tsp ground ginger
- 7oz/200g/1 cup pumpkin puree (either canned, or buy a fresh pumpkin and make your own
- 1¼ tsp bicarbonate of soda
- ½ tsp salt
- 6fl oz/180ml/¾ cup buttermilk

For the filling

- 900ml double cream
- 6 egg yolks
- 210g light brown sugar
- 3oz chopped pecans
- 1oz salted butter

An arctic roll with a bit of zing... Perfect for Halloween parties.

To make the pumpkin puree...

Cut a pumpkin in half and scoop out the seeds and pulp, and remove the skin. Dice the pumpkin flesh into small cubes, and either steam or boil until tender. Place in a bowl and mash or puree using a blender.

Method

Preheat your oven to 170°c (160°c fan)/325°f/GM 3 and grease a large baking sheet. Cream together the butter and sugar, then add the egg a bit at a time, stirring well to make a smooth, curdle-free mixture.

Put the flour, cinnamon, ginger, nutmeg, bicarbonate of soda and salt into a sieve, and have the buttermilk and pumpkin puree to hand. Sieve half the flour mix into the butter mix and fold in gently. Add half the buttermilk and half the pumpkin puree, and mix well. Add the crushed pecans, and mix well.

Pipe (or dollop) the batter into 2" diameter rounds and smooth off with the back of a spoon. Bake in the oven for 10-12 minutes.

- If opting to decorate the whoopies with fondant icing bats and witches etc, do so before adding the filling.

To make the pecan ice cream...

To ensure it will be set, make the ice cream the day before. Put the cream in a pan and bring slowly to the boil, stirring ocassionally. Reduce the heat, add the sugar and stir well to dissolve, then leave to cool slightly. Melt the butter in a frying pan, add the pecans and toast gently for 2-3 minutes. Leave to cool. Put the egg yolks in a bowl and whisk, then pour the cream on top, stirring constantly, and add the toasted pecans. Put into the freezer for at least 5 hours to set.

47

October

Honeyed parsnip and rosemary whoopie pie

Makes approximately 16
Preparation: 30 minutes
Cooking: 10 minutes
Total: 40 minutes

Ingredients

- 8oz/225g/1¾ cups plain flour
- 1 tsp bicarbonate of soda
- 2.5oz/75g/¼ cup (½ stick) butter
- 7fl oz/200ml/¾ cup buttermilk
- 1 medium egg
- 7oz/200g/1½ cups large diced parsnip
- 4 tsp clear (runny) honey (plus a little extra to glaze the parsnip)

For the filling

- 7oz/200g/¾ cup cream cheese
- 2 tsp dried rosemary
- 1 tsp clear (runny) honey

As the cold nights draw in, turn up the heat with the intense, warming flavours of parsnip and rosemary.

Method

Preheat your oven to 170°c (160°c fan)/325°f/GM 3 and grease a large baking sheet.

First dice the parsnip into large pieces of about 1". Place on a baking tray, glaze each piece with a little honey and place in the oven. After 10 minutes, turn the pieces over and bake for a further 10 minutes until soft and tender. Once cooked, put the pieces into a mixing bowl with 2 teaspoons of cold water and whizz to a puree with a hand blender.

Sift the flour and bicarbonate of soda on top of the parsnip puree, then add all the other ingredients. Mix well with an electric hand whisk or wooden spoon until you have a smooth, thick batter.

Pipe (or dollop) the whoopie pie batter into 2" diameter rounds, then bake in the oven for 10-12 minutes, or until they spring back when lightly touched.

When cooked, take out of the oven and leave to cool in the tray for 5 minutes, before transferring to a wire rack.

To make the filling...

Crumble the dried rosemary into the cream cheese, add the honey and mix well.

Why not try...

Making extra parsnip puree and adding some to the cream cheese for a more intense flavour?

49

November

Apple and cinnamon whoopie pie

Makes approximately 18
Preparation: 20 minutes
Cooking: 10 minutes
Total: 30 minutes

Ingredients

- 4.5oz/130g/½ cup (1 stick) butter
- 7oz/200g/1 cup castor sugar
- 1 medium egg, beaten
- 14oz/395g/3 cups plain flour
- 1 tsp cinnamon
- 1¼ tsp bicarbonate of soda
- ½ tsp salt
- 9fl oz/270ml/1 cup buttermilk

For the filling

- 7oz/200g/1 cup mascarpone cheese
- 5oz/150g/1½ cup peeled, cored and diced apple
- 1 tbsp lemon juice

Delicious as mini whoopies, the refreshing apple puree blends with warming cinnamon to help stave off those chilly nights.

Method

Preheat your oven to 170°c (160°c fan)/325°f/GM 3 and grease a large baking sheet.

Cream together the butter and sugar, then add the egg a bit at a time, stirring well to make a smooth, curdle-free mixture.

Put the flour, cinnamon, bicarbonate of soda and salt into a sieve, and have the buttermilk to hand. Sieve half the flour mixture into the butter mixture and fold in gently. Add half the buttermilk and mix well.

Continue until all flour and buttermilk is folded in and you have a smooth, thick batter.

Pipe (or dollop) the whoopie pie batter into 2" diameter rounds and smooth off with the back of a spoon.

Bake in the oven for 10-12 minutes, or until they spring back when lightly touched. When cooked, take out of the oven and leave to cool in the tray for 5 minutes, before transferring to a wire rack.

To make the apple mascarpone filling...

Peel and core the apples, then dice into small chunks. Place the chunks in a saucepan with 1 tbsp water, and cook gently for 10-15 minutes, or until the apple is soft.

Drain any excess water, whizz with a blender, then put the apple puree into the mascarpone, along with the lemon juice, and mix well.

November

Jalapeño, cheese and guacamole whoopie pie

Makes approximately 16
Preparation: 20 minutes
Cooking: 10 minutes
Total: 30 minutes

Ingredients

- 4 slices of green jalapeño pepper, finely diced
- 2oz/50g/½ cup grated cheese
- 8oz/225g/1¾ cups plain flour
- 1 tsp bicarbonate of soda
- 2.5oz/75g/¼ cup (½ stick) butter
- 8.5fl oz/250ml/1 cup soured cream
- 1 medium egg

For the filling

- 2 ripe avocados
- 2 tbsp soured cream
- 1 clove crushed garlic
- 1 tsp lime juice
- Handful of fresh chopped coriander (cilantro)
- Salt and pepper to taste

Light up your tastebuds with these fiery fancies.

Method

Preheat your oven to 170°c (160°c fan)/325°f/GM 3 and grease a large baking sheet.

Grate the cheese into a large mixing bowl, and add the chopped jalapeños.

Sift the flour and bicarbonate of soda on top of the cheese and jalapeños, then add all the other ingredients.

Mix well with an electric hand whisk or wooden spoon until you have a smooth, thick batter.

Pipe (or dollop) the whoopie pie batter into 2" diameter rounds, and bake in the oven for 10-12 minutes, or until they spring back when lightly touched.

When cooked, take out of the oven and leave to cool in the tray for 5 minutes, before transferring to a wire rack.

To make the filling...

Mash the avocado, then add all the other ingredients and mix well.

Why not try...

Adding some finely grated lime zest to the whoopie pie batter?

52

December

Rum and raisin whoopie pie

Makes approximately 18
Preparation: 20 minutes
Cooking: 10 minutes
Total: 30 minutes

Ingredients

- 4.5oz/130g/½ cup (1 stick) butter
- 7oz/200g/1 cup castor sugar
- 1 medium egg, beaten
- 11oz/310g/2½ cups plain flour
- 3oz/85g/½ cup cocoa powder
- 1¼ tsp bicarbonate of soda
- ½ tsp salt
- 8fl oz/240ml/1 cup buttermilk
- 1fl oz/30ml dark rum
- 7oz/200g/1½ cups (packed) raisins

For the filling

- 4oz/115g/½ cup (1 stick) unsalted butter
- 8oz/225g/2 cups (unsifted) icing sugar
- 1 tbsp milk
- ½ tsp vanilla essence

A (slightly) grown-up whoopie with dark, delectable rum to bring out the festive feeling.

Method

Preheat your oven to 170°c (160°c fan)/325°f/GM 3 and grease a large baking sheet.

Cream together the butter and sugar, then add the egg a bit at a time, stirring well to make a smooth, curdle-free mixture. Put the flour, cocoa, bicarbonate of soda and salt into a sieve, and have the buttermilk and dark rum to hand.

Sieve half the flour mixture into the butter mixture and fold in gently. Add half the buttermilk and half the dark rum and mix well. Continue until all flour, buttermilk and rum is folded in, and you have a smooth, thick batter, then add the raisins and mix well.

Pipe (or dollop) the whoopie pie batter into 2" diameter rounds and smooth off with the back of a spoon. Bake in the oven for 10-12 minutes, or until they spring back when lightly touched.

When cooked, take out of the oven and leave to cool in the tray for 5 minutes, before transferring to a wire rack.

To make the vanilla buttercream filling...

Beat the butter with a wooden spoon or electric whisk until light and creamy, then add about half the icing sugar, and mix in well.

Tip the rest of the icing sugar into the bowl, mix and continue to beat until the buttercream is pale and creamy. Add the milk and vanilla, and mix well.

December

Brie and cranberry whoopie pie

Makes approximately 16
Preparation: 10 minutes
Cooking: 10 minutes
Total: 20 minutes

Ingredients

- 8oz/225g/1¾ cups plain flour
- 1 tsp bicarbonate of soda
- 2.5oz/75g/¼ cup (½ stick) butter
- 7fl oz/200ml/¾ cup buttermilk
- 1 medium egg
- 2oz/50g/½ cup dried cranberries
- 2 tsp cranberry sauce

For the filling

- 14oz/400g sliced brie

These cranberry-packed whoopies make a delicious accompaniment to any Christmas spread.

Method

Preheat your oven to 170°c (160°c fan)/325°f/ GM 3 and grease a large baking sheet.

Sift the flour and bicarbonate of soda into a large mixing bowl, then add all the other ingredients.

Mix well with an electric hand whisk or wooden spoon until you have a smooth, thick batter.

Pipe (or dollop) the whoopie pie batter into 2" diameter rounds and smooth off with a spoon.

Bake in the oven for 10-12 minutes, or until they spring back when lightly touched.

When cooked, take out of the oven and leave to cool in the tray for 5 minutes, before transferring to a wire rack.

For the filling...

Slice the brie, and sandwich between two whoopie halves.

Why not try...

Adding some crushed walnuts to the brie for an extra festive touch?

56

Whoopie Pie Filling Recipes

In addition to the filling flavours included with each whoopie pie recipe, there are many others that you may want to try – including some that require no preparation at all. The possibilities are almost endless, but I've included a few ideas below to get you started on your experiments – divided into sweet and savoury sections.

Alternative Sweet Fillings

No prep fillings which taste great on their own in whoopies:

- Peanut butter
- Chocolate spread
- Peanut butter and honey or jam (that's jelly to US readers!)
- Cream cheese/mascarpone
- Clotted cream
- Butter and jam
- Ice-cream – all flavours. For extra decadence, crush one of your favourite chocolate bars/treats (Flake, Maltesers, M&Ms etc) and add to the ice cream – just don't think about the calories!
- Marshmallow fluff - from a tub (widely available in stores throughout the US - readers outside North America however, can buy this online). Alternatively make from scratch: see January sweet original whoopie on page 10 for recipe details. Although there are other recipes, which call for icing/confectioners' sugar, this is by far the simplest.

Fillings that require a little prep

Start with your base filling (plain buttercream, mascarpone or cream cheese) then add different flavour ingredients to create your own individual whoopie pie fillings. Flavour suggestions and quantities follow the base recipes.

Standard Plain buttercream
Ingredients
4oz/115g/½ cup (1 stick) unsalted butter 8oz/225g/2 cups (unsifted) icing sugar
1 tbsp milk

Beat the butter until creamy, with either a wooden spoon or electric whisk.
Gradually beat the icing sugar into the butter, and continue beating until light and creamy.
Mix in the milk and vanilla.

Note: for a vegan alternative, substitute butter for soya margarine, and milk for soya cream.

Plain mascarpone

Ingredients
7oz/200g/¾ cup mascarpone

Plain cream cheese

Ingredients
7oz/200g/¾ cup cream cheese

Note: for a vegan alternative to cream cheese, try Sheese in the UK, or in the US Soymage or VeganRella.

Sweet Filling Flavour Table
Note: if you use standard plain buttercream as your base filling, leave out the milk/soya cream if the chosen flavour includes liquid or pureed ingredients. A (v) after the title denotes the filling is (or can easily be) vegan.

Flavour	Method
Almond and Cider (v)	Boil ¼ pt/120ml/½ cup cider with 2tbsp castor sugar for 5 minutes. Leave to cool. Add 2oz/55g/⅔ cup toasted, flaked almonds to base filling, along with 1tbsp cider syrup. Note: any leftover cider syrup can be placed in a jar in the fridge and used in other recipes.
Amaretto Cream	Add 1tbsp amaretto to base filling for a powerful punch!
Bailey's	Add 1tbsp Bailey's Irish Cream to the base filling.
Blueberry (v)	2oz/55g/⅓ cup fresh blueberries – force through a sieve as for strawberry puree (see page 30). Add 1tbsp blueberry puree to base filling.
Brandy (v)	Add 1tbsp brandy to base filling.
Cinnamon (v)	Add ½tsp cinnamon to base filling.
Coconut (v)	Add 2oz/55g/⅔ cup desiccated coconut
Double Chocolate chip (v – use vegan chocolate chips)	Add 1tbsp cocoa powder, and 1oz/30g/⅓ cup chocolate chips
Chocolate, honey and hazelnut	Add 1oz/30g/⅓ cup chocolate chips, 1oz/30g/⅓ cup crushed hazelnuts and 1 tbsp clear (runny) honey.
Chocolate and mint (v)	Add 1 tbsp cocoa powder, and 2tsp finely chopped mint.
Lemon or lime (or both!) (v)	Add 1 tbsp of juice, and finely grated zest.

59

Maltesers	Crush about 2oz/55g of Maltesers (you can use more or less, depending how intensely Malteserish you want your filling!) and add to your base filling.
Mango (v)	Either puree a fresh mango in a blender, or use 1tbsp fresh mango juice (not from concentrate). Add to chosen base filling.
Mango and Lime (v)	Add 1tsp fresh lime juice, and 2tsp fresh mango juice (not from concentrate) to base filling.
Mint (v)	Add 2tsp finely chopped mint
Mixed Christmas Spice (v)	Add a pinch of each of the following, plus 1 clove: nutmeg; cinnamon; ginger. Note: remove the clove once mixing is complete – and do not use the blade attachment of a blender to mix this filling, or it will result in bitter clove bits spread throughout.
Mocha (v)	1tsp cocoa powder, and 1tsp instant coffee mixed with 1tsp water. Mix well into base filling.
Pomegranate (v)	1tbsp fresh pomegranate juice, plus 2oz/55g/⅓ cup fresh pomegranate seeds
Pear and almond (v)	Peel, core and dice 2 dessert pears. Stew in a saucepan with 1tbsp water for a few minutes, till soft. Mash to a puree, then add 1 tbsp of the pear puree to your base filling along with a few drops of almond essence (to taste)
Vanilla (v)	Add ½tsp vanilla extract (or 1-2 drops if using vanilla flavouring)

Alternative Savoury Fillings

No prep fillings which taste great on their own in whoopies:

All the cheeses work amazingly: cheddar; mozzarella; feta; cream cheese; ricotta; blue cheeses; goats cheese; sheep cheese; jarlsberg; emmental; fruit cheddars; brie; camembert; fried haloumi
Sliced tomato or cucumber
Raw, thinly slice red/white/spring onion
Sliced smoked salmon with a little lemon juice and black pepper
Smoked mackerel fillet, lightly mashed with a fork
Meat pates or pastes
Sliced meats: ham; beef; chicken; turkey
Deli meats: chorizo; salami; haslet; corned beef; pastrami